A MEMORIALL OF BAIRD

Gaelic: Mac a'Bhàird

Debra Baird
Isaac Baird
Branton Baird

BOOK COVER
Heather Baird Snyder, BFA
Graphic Designer, Artist
Editor of "The Gryphon" newsletter for Clan Baird Society Worldwide, Inc.
hsnyder65@yahoo.com

Dr. Debra BAIRD, BS, MA, Ph.D., FSA Scot
Genealogist, Author, Academic, Professor
President Clan Baird Society Worldwide, Inc.
www.clanbairdsociety.com
djbaird4@gmail.com

Mr. Isaac S BAIRD, BS, FSA Scot
Genealogist, Risk Analyst, Seanchaidh
2nd Vice President Clan Baird Society Worldwide, Inc.
iandsbaird@outlook.com

Mr. Branton B BAIRD, BS, MA, M.S, ABD
Linguist, Author, Academic, Professor
South Eastern U.S.A. Commissioner, Clan Baird Society Worldwide, Inc.
brantonbaird@icloud.com

Copyright 2020 by Debra J Baird, Isaac S Baird, and Branton B Baird

All rights reserved. No part of this book may be reproduced in any form or by any electronic or mechanical means, including information storage and retrieval systems, without permission in writing from the publisher, except by a reviewer, who may quote brief passages in a review. Scanning, uploading, and electronic distribution of this book or the facilitation of such without the permission of the publisher is prohibited. Please purchase only authorized electronic editions, and do not participate in or encourage electronic piracy of copyrighted materials. Your support of the author's rights is appreciated. Any member of educational institutions wishing to photocopy part or all of the work for classroom use, or anthology, should send inquiries to SaintMauricePublishing, 3487 County Road 3459, Haleyville, Alabama, 35565.

First edition published April 2020 by
SaintMauricePublishing
Haleyville, Alabama

Published in the United States of America

Baird, Debra J, Baird, Isaac S, Baird, Branton B

Includes bibliographical references and index.
ISBN: 978-0-99808-50-8-1
1. Clan Baird—History. I. Title

Library of Congress Control Number: 2020937259

SaintMauricePublishing
Haleyville, Alabama, 35565

http://www.SaintMauricePublishing.com

Sword of Destiny

A MEMORIALL OF BAIRD (*Gaelic: Mac a'Bhàird*)

TABLE OF CONTENTS

Title Page
Author's Page
Dr. Bruce Durie Quote   v
Commanders' Forward   vi
Photograph of Richard Holman-Baird
Photograph of Richard's Family, Amelia, Richard,
Polly and Angus   vii

Early Records of Baird/Mac a 'Bh*à*ird//Bard/Beard/Beaird	3
The Baird Beginnings, Cambusnethan in Lanark	8
Chart of Baird Movement in Scotland Over Time	12
Biggar, Lanarkshire Bairds	13
The Gartsherries	16
The Ordinhivas Bairds	20
The Posso Bairds	23
The Auchmedden Bairds	24
The Newbyths	27
The Saughtonhalls	29
Bairds Have Never Been Part of Another Clan, nor a Sept	30
Bairds Are Considered a Clan Under a Chief of Name and Arms	30
Warrant from the Lord Lyon	32
Arms and Armigers	33
DNA	35
A Baird Bibliography	37
The Baird Crest	41

Humbly sheweth:

1. That Baird (*Gaelic: Mac a'Bhàird*) and its variant spellings was of old considered separate from any Clan or Chief
2. That Baird (*Gaelic: Mac a'Bhàird*) and its variant spellings are not part of any other Clan or Family
3. That there is an expressed will of Bairds to be considered a Clan or Family, and to have a Chief of Name and Arms.

Some are born Chiefs, some become Chiefs, and some have Chiefship thrust upon them...

Dr. Bruce Durie PhD QG

FORWARD

Richard Holman-Baird of Rickarton, Ury, and Lochwood, Commander of Clan Baird

Our thanks must go to Isaac Baird, Branton Baird and his mother, Debra, for putting together such a comprehensive Baird History. I have, personally, learnt a lot more about my own roots than I knew before I opened its covers! It is well researched and should be a compulsory read for all Bairds.

As your newly elected Commander, I hope I manage to live up to everybody's expectations and can take Clan Baird forward to greater times for the future.

Best regards
Richard

Photo Above: Richard on a stalking hunt, Glendessary

Photo at Left: Daughter Amelia, Richard, his wife Polly, and son Angus, attending the Queen. Notice that Angus is wearing his Baird trews. Richard is a member of the Royal Company of Archers, currently known as the Queen's Bodyguard For Scotland. Richard is called upon to guard the Queen when she is in Scotland.

Early Records of Baird/ Mac a 'Bhàird /Barde/Bard/Beard/Beaird

There are multiple suggested origins to the surname Baird which include a French-Germanic origin, Briton (Welsh/Cumbric), and Gaelic/Celt origin. Most of the family leans toward the Cumbric and Gaelic/Celt origin, due to their own more recent experience. Origins are not well delineated by DNA results that have been gathered over time.

Written records of family feats and land ownership do not appear until the 11th century, with the use of de Barde as the surname, but in England. This origination claim is that the Bairds, as de Bardes, came to the British Isles with William the Conqueror from the south of France, in 1066, or closely thereafter. This claim made by many prominent families of the United Kingdom, is of course highly desirable. In most cases it is not true.

It also is possible that Bairds arrived in Scotland with William the Lyon, upon his return in 1174, since documents naming them in Lanarkshire began to appear shortly thereafter, and family origination stories begin with tales of valor concerning saving William the Lyon. In fact, the main myth of Bairds obtaining land and titles comes from the act of one Baird who reportedly saved King William from a wild boar, while they were out hunting, using only one arrow. This was a very lucky shot, one might say.

As mentioned with the use of the Mac a'Bhaird Gaelic name, (Mac an Bhaird in Ireland) there is also the theory that Bairds were originally Britons, and originated in Cumbria which later became Lanarkshire. In this theory, the occupational name Bardd (Welsh) existed for generations before William the Conqueror or William the Lyon. This would explain why ancient Scottish Baird family documents began in Lanarkshire, close to modern day Glasgow, and why Baird DNA results are heavily Brittonic with Germanic admixture.

A proposed Gaelic origin of the surname states that the name has been anglicized from its original Gaelic form as Gaelic receded from Scotland in the 13th through 15th century. The use of the Gaelic Mac a'Bhàird derives first from Ireland, from Ulster, as Mac an Bhaird, a very learned family of hereditary bards, and then appears in Scotland as the Gaels moved into the mainland of Scotland. The current word "Bard", in the English and Scottish lexicon is recognized as deriving from the Gaelic word "Bard"[1] meaning a poet and can be seen in Scottish Parliamentary records in 1450.[2] These Bards and later Bairds are known for their creative use of language and love of education. Even until the loss of the estate of Auchmedden, the Laird had an extensive library that was widely used for reference by many of the well-educated of that era.

Baird families remain in Scotland, but currently there are more Bairds outside Scotland than in, primarily in the United States, but also in Canada, Australia, and New Zealand. The modern Baird Clan and Family is a part of the worldwide Scottish Diaspora that began in the 16th century, due to religion, conflicts over monarchs, the later Highland Clearances, and the extreme middle-class poverty of Scottish cities in the 19th-20th centuries.

Many believe that the Bairds are not highlanders, but only an ancient lowland Family, rather than a Clan. The Bairds themselves consider that they are both, an amalgamation of highlanders and lowlanders. This is evidenced in that the Bairds retained a chief named from the Ordinhivas/Auchmedden branch but have not had a

---

[1] Alexander MacBain. *An Etymological dictionary of the Gaelic language*. Stirling. Eneas Mackay: Stirling, 1911, p 30.
[2] *The Records of the Parliaments of Scotland to 1707*, K.M. Brown et al eds (St Andrews, 2007-2019), 1450/1/11. Date accessed: 19 July 2019.

recorded chief for more than three hundred years ("Arms were recorded in 1672 for Sir James Baird of Auchmeddan and since then there have been a number of Baird recordings but none appears to suggest that any were representer of the house of Baird and thus Lyon would require some evidence of that position")[3]. The first Baird called "our chief" in family documents was Walter Baird of Ordinhivas, the father of Lillias Baird, who married her cousin, Gilbert Baird of Auchmedden. The DNA of Bairds show that most are a mixture of Norman-Cumbric-Celtic-Germanic ancient ancestry.

According to William, 7th Laird of Auchmedden, who spent his final years in his brother-in-law's house, Alexander Duff, Lord Fife, in Aberdeen, the beginnings of the Bairds in the British Islands were as he wrote circa 1770.

> *The Sirname of BAIRD is originally of the South of France, where there were several Families of it in the reign of Louis IV, and it is said are still, but the first of the name mentioned in Britain came from Normandy to England with William the Conqueror. And from the time when it first appears in Scotland, there is reason to believe that some of that name came here with King William the Lyon, when he returned from his captivity in England, anno 1174, as it is agreed by all our historians, several English gentlemen did. For it is certain that in less than sixty years after that period, they possessed fine estates, and had made good alliances in the South and South West counties of Scotland.*[4]

---

[3] Elizabeth Roads, Snawdoun Herald, *Email Letter Concerning the Name Baird*, 4 October 2017.

[4] William N. Fraser, *An Account of the Surname of Baird: particularly of the families of Auchmedden, Newbyth and Saughtonhall*. Stevens: Edinburgh, 1857, p 6

There are four recognized main modern branches, the Gartsherries, who are considered the remnant line of the original Cambusnethan Bairds, the first Scottish Bairds mentioned in documents, from Biggar, Lanarkshire, in the 12th century, with the later divisions of Posso, Ordinhivas, Auchmedden, Saughtonhall, and Newbyth descending from the Cambusnethans.[5] Very little has been kept of the written history of the Bairds, either by design of the historian (a cousin said Bairds would hold a grudge forever, even against a brother), by the destruction of materials by family or enemies, or by the natural destruction of records by the toll of years in diaspora.

It is a great providence that William Baird, 7th Laird of Auchmedden, in his years of Aberdeen exile after the Rising of the '45, wrote what he knew of the family history, although his information is obviously skewed and has only the history as he wished it to be. Matters were made worse when a grandson by his daughter Henrietta, William N. Fraser, published an edited and redacted edition of his work, with much information from the original manuscript removed or changed. The Lairds of Auchmedden are probably not extinct, as many believe, since the fates of three of their sons and one daughter are lost in the mists of movement to the American Colonies in the late 18th century. The Auchmeddens were the main branch of the later Saughtonhalls and Newbyths, baronies created very recently indeed, for a much younger son of the Laird of Auchmedden. There are also many branches of this family that were from other younger sons of several Lairds of that name over time, so the claims that the Auchmeddens are extinct is not accurate.

The challenge has been that the heirs of that line have been very difficult to identify. It is posited that this problem stems from the

---

[5] https://www.clanbairdsociety.com/society-officers, retrieved August 12, 2018.

fate of William 7th of Auchmedden, and his participation in the Jacobite Revolt of 1745, as well as his insistence on remaining Catholic in a time when it was illegal to be so. It is also posited that he dabbled in being a part of the recognized Church, but proofs are not evident. As continues to be the way of the world, when a person is involved in a losing cause, and there is extreme restitution demanded by the winners, family members disperse quickly. This was certainly true for William, the 7th Laird, who had some particular enemies that wished to destroy anything related to the Auchmedden Baird family. Alexander Garden of Troup (1714-1785), was the nemesis of William. He made sure the Bairds of Auchmedden were removed from the map of the Buchan Coast, or as much as was possible.

In order to do this, Alexander Garden of Troup personally supervised the pulling down of the manor house at the Mains of Auchmedden. He also saw to the final destruction of what was left of the castle on this site. He had been kidnapped and held hostage during the '45 by Jacobites[6] and according to oral sources, blamed William Baird of Auchmedden for this action. His hatred for William Baird the 7th Laird caused him to see to the removal of the name Auchmedden from many parts of the old estate. In 1719, their respective fathers had come together to build a bridge across Dubstan Brae. "The small stone bridge at the foot of Dubstan Brae near Nethermill farm, at the border between Gamrie and Aberdour, is built as a joint effort between the Laird of Troup and the Laird of Auchmedden."[7] The Mill of Auchmedden, being within sight of Garden's home at Troup, was given a forced name change to the Nethermill, which it holds today.

---

[6] http://www.discovergardenstown.co.uk/1700sa.htm, retrieved 19 February 2019
[7] Ibid

The Baird Beginnings, Cambusnethan in Lanark

The first Baird mentioned in documents in what is now Great Britain, was Le Seigneur de Barde, who was named as one of William Duke of Normandy's men in the conquest of England. He was never listed as being in Scotland. This mention is in a History of Normandy, held in the Advocates Library, and in Hollingshead's Chronicle, Library of Glasgow.[8] The mention gives some validity to William, 7th of Auchmedden's claim that the Bairds came to Britain in 1066 or shortly thereafter with William the Conqueror but does not prove Le Seigneur Barde is the progenitor of the Scottish Bairds.

The first mention of Bairds in Scotland is in 1178, when Henry de Barde serves as witness to a charter granted by King William the Lyon to the Bishop of Glasgow, concerning some lands in Stirling. Again, legend gives us the story that a Baird returned with King William from his captivity in England. The story explaining the boar on the coat of arms of Bairds is due to a Baird lost to history who reportedly saved King William the Lyon from being killed by a wild boar while hunting. We do not know if this is the same Baird who came back from England with him. It is said that it only took one arrow for Baird to kill the boar, thus he was either very lucky or an excellent archer.

From 1202-1228, Henry de Barde further witnessed charters of others. Following this mention, the Ragman's Roll from 1292 and forward, carries several Barde/Baird names who swore allegiance to King Edward I of England, those being, Fergus de Baird of Meikle and Little Kyp, John Bard of Evandale, and Robert Baird of Cambusnethan.[9] The Ragman's Roll of 1296 shows four Bairds, to

---

[8] *The Chartulary of Glasgow*, Scotch College at Paris.
[9] *Ragman's Rolls Index*, as published by the Bannatyne Club, Edinburgh, 1834.

wit, Duncan Bard of Striuelin, Fergus Bard of Lanark, Johan Bard of Lanark, and Nicol Bard of Lanark. Also, a charter was granted to Richard Baird of Meikle and Little Kyp in Lanarkshire in the 13th century and King Robert the Bruce granted the barony of Cambusnethan to a Robert Baird, after the Wars of Independence.

    This Robert Baird built what we know as the "Baird Tower". These Bairds were wealthy and owned extensive lands, including the Barony of Avondale. The tower seems to have been the only place to offer human accommodation until at least 1490. Robert Baird must have switched allegiance during the reign of David II, supporting the campaign of Edward Balliol to gain the Scottish Crown, and lost his claims to the lands.[10] 'The Memorie' of the Somervilles gives a description of the Baird Tower as thus: 20 feet square and 4 storeys high, so slightly smaller in dimension than Hallbar, which is nearby. It had rooms on each floor, and the 4th may have been used by the lady and children of Robert Baird.

    According to J. Malcolm Bulloch the branches of Auchmedden, Newbyth and Saughton seem to stem from Lanarkshire. In his words, "the cradle of the Baird family".[11] This indicates that those who remained in Lanarkshire, for this work's purpose, the Gartsherries, were by place and time, the original stock, where the original name was spelled "Bard" or "Barde". This information was taken by Bulloch from the work of William of Auchmedden, 7th Laird.

> [Auchmedden, New Byth and Sauchton]," have long been familiar to genealogists in the shape of two transcripts, neither well edited, issued in 1857 and 1870. It seems as if

---

[10] Gordon W. Mason, *The Castles of Glasgow and Clyde*. 2nd ed. Goblinshead, 2014, p. 167.
[11] J. Malcolm Bulloch, *The Bairds of Auchmedden and Strichen, Aberdeenshire*. Buchan Club, Peterhead: Scotland, 1934, p 3.

Lanarkshire were the cradle of the Baird family, whose original name is spelt variously as Bard and Barde. William Baird tells us that the spelling "Baird" did not appear till the end of the sixteenth century, but the pronunciation "Bard" persisted until comparatively recent times. This is neither the time nor the place — nor have I the necessary knowledge — to attempt to connect the first Bairds of Auchmedden with a Lanarkshire origin. William Baird himself was very vague about it, and his genealogical successors have not been able to throw much light on the subject. The Gartsherrie group were equally at sea.

The Lanarkshire group is the first we hear of, for in 1240 a charter was granted in favour of Richard Baird of the lands of Little and Meikle Kyp in Lanarkshire. In 1306 Robert the Bruce granted a charter of the Barony of Cambusnethan, in what is now Wishaw, in favour of Robert de Barde; Cambusnethan was lost to the family in 1345 by the forfeiture of Sir Robert Barde, who was succeeded by the Somervilles.

William Baird's story was that the Cambusnethan group, besides losing their lands, petered out in one heiress who married a Stewart of Darnley. Migration of the Lanarkshire Bairds then set on. One group, we are told by William Baird, moved northwards to Ross-shire as lairds of Indety and Balmaduthy; and in the fifteenth century one Lanarkshire Baird, having quarrelled with a neighbour, is said to have been given sanctuary by the Earl of Huntly, who granted him land in the Forest of Boyne, five centuries ago, in 1430. The Boyne group ultimately settled at Ordinhivas, or Ordinhuiff, which is now merged with the Seafield estates in the parish of Fordyce. One of them, George Baird of Ordinhivas (d. 1557), who was sheriff depute of Aberdeenshire from 1531 to 1535, and is dealt with in

Littlejohn's "Aberdeenshire Sheriff Court" (i. 441-2), is vaguely described as "great-great-grandson of James Baird of the family of Cambusnethan." By his wife Janet Fraser, said to have belonged to the Philorth family, he had a son Walter, who married Catherine."[12]

The documentation points to the Cambusnethans as the first Baird group in Scotland, and the origination point of all other Bairds of Scotland over time. Although William Baird, 7th of Auchmedden desperately tried to distance his family from the Cambusnethan Bairds, it simply is not possible that the Posso Bairds, and thus the Auchmeddens, simply "sprang from the heather" without any ties to earlier generations. Lost in history is the direct Cambusnethan link to Andrew Baird who bought the lands of Auchmedden from John, Earl of Buchan on 10 November 1534. [13]

---

[12] J. Malcolm Bulloch, *The Bairds of Auchmedden and Strichen, Aberdeenshire*. Buchan Club, Peterhead: Scotland, 1934,
p 3-4.
[13] Ibid.

CHART OF BAIRD MOVEMENT IN SCOTLAND OVER TIME

Biggar Lanarkshire Bairds

Lands given for saving William the Lyon from a wild boar. Henry de Barde, as Mariscallus apud Strivelin, first documented Baird as witness in 1178 to a charter of lands in Stirling by King William to the Bishop of Glasgow. Richard Baird of Meikle and Little Kyp was granted land in Lanarkshire in 1240.

Cambusnethan Gartsherrie Bairds

Richard Baird of Meikle and Little Kyp likely had several sons and they remained in Lanarkshire for generations, according to the book *The Bairds of Gartsherrie* and *the manuscript of William Baird, 7th of Auchmedden*. Some of those descendants lived and farmed in Old Monkland, first on the farm of Kirkwood and then High Cross, before expanding into Coal and Iron works.
Robert Baird was the Sheriff of Lanark in 1329 and was given the barony of Cambusnethan from King Robert the Bruce. The modern Gartsherrie Bairds are the remaining estate holders in Scotland, and owned Auchmedden last, from 1854-1925.

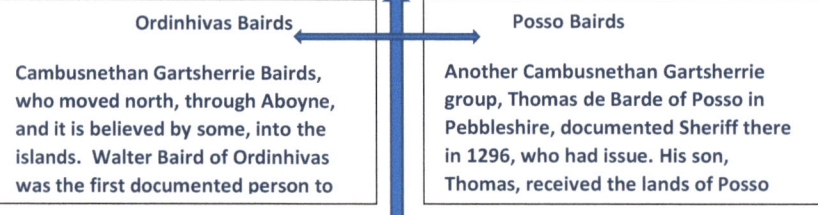

Ordinhivas Bairds	Posso Bairds
Cambusnethan Gartsherrie Bairds, who moved north, through Aboyne, and it is believed by some, into the islands. Walter Baird of Ordinhivas was the first documented person to	Another Cambusnethan Gartsherrie group, Thomas de Barde of Posso in Pebbleshire, documented Sheriff there in 1296, who had issue. His son, Thomas, received the lands of Posso

Auchmedden Bairds

Part of the Bairds given lands in the north. from Aboyne to the sea, in 1430 by the Earl of Huntley, flourished in Banff and Aberdeenshire until 1746, when the estates were sold to pay debts incurred for Bonnie Prince Charlie. The Ordinhivas Bairds married into the Posso and Auchmedden's, bringing the two groups back together.

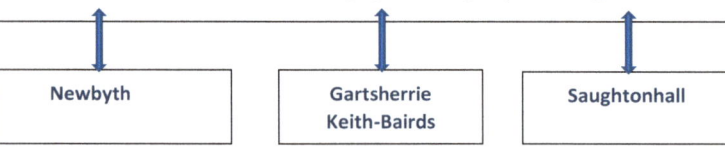

Newbyth	Gartsherrie Keith-Bairds	Saughtonhall

Notes for Table on Previous Page:
Although many modern Bairds (and ancient ones) have tried to draw charts that exclude one family branch or another, there is absolutely no documented evidence that all Bairds in Scotland did not originate from the Lanarkshire Biggar Group. While DNA analysis is very informative and very helpful, it cannot yet determine exactly who the Bairds are, due to many name changes in the form of the ancient practice of fostering distant relatives and giving them the name of the main house, or clan members simply taking on the name, giving their fealty to the chief.

Biggar, Lanarkshire Bairds

Henry de Barde served as Mariscallus apud Strivelin and was the first documented Scottish Baird as witness in 1178 to a charter of lands in Stirling by King William to the Bishop of Glasgow. Richard Baird of Meikle and Little Kyp was granted lands in Lanarkshire in 1240. Lanarkshire was the beginning, and there is very little documentation of these earliest Bairds.

William Baird, 7th Laird of Auchmedden, outlined what he knew of them.[14]

- 1066: Le Seigneur de Barde, mentioned as one of William Duke of Normandy's followers in the conquest of England. (A large old History of Normandy in the Advocates' Library, and *Hollingshead's Chronicle,* who calls him Seigneur de Beart.) *Library of Glasgow*
- 1143: William Baird, made Bishop of Durham, by King William Rufus, *Anglia Sacra,* pp. 712 and 718, tome 1.

---

[14] William N. Fraser, *An Account of the Surname of Baird: particularly of the families of Auchmedden, Newbyth and Saughtonhall*. Stevens: Edinburgh, 1857, p 3.

1178: Henry de Barde, Mariscallus apud Strivelin, witness to a charter granted by King William the Lion Heart to the Bishop of Glasgow, upon some lands in the town of Stirling, *The Chartulary of Glasgow, sent lately from the Scotch College at Paris.*

1194: Winchester, April 17 In a safe conduct granted by King Richard I to King William the Lion, in which large appointments of money and provisions during his going and coming and stay in England are ordered for him, Hugo de Baird is one of the subscribing witnesses. *Rymer's Foemdera,* v 1, p. 88.

1224: Magistrus Riccardus de Barde, witness to a charter granted by the Bishop of Glasgow Chartulary.

1228: Richard de Baird makes a donation to the Abbot and Convent of Kelso, dated at Lismahago, and the signing witnesses are William de Maitland, ancestor of the Earl of Lauderdale, Archibald Lord Douglas, William Fleming, ancestor to the Earl of Wigton, Malcom Lockhart, &c *Chartulary of Kelso, p. 160.*

1233: Robert Baird. - *Chartulary of Paisley.*

1240: Richard. -Ibid.

1240: May 26, King Alexander II, confirms a donation made by Richard de Baud to the Monastery of Kelso, Rudulf de Dundas and Walter son of Allan, Justiciarius Scotiae witnesses, Douglas Baronage.

1240: Robert, son of Waldevus de Biggar, grants a charter to Richard Baird, upon the lands of Little and Meikle Kyp in the County of Lanark. *Dalrymple's Collections*, p. 397 and *Nisbet's Heraldry.*

1270: Peter Bulkeley, second son to Robert Bulkeley, by a daughter of Butler of Bewsey in Lancashire, married the daughter of --Baird. Robert Bulkeley, ancestor of this family, was Lord of the Manor of Bulkeley in the county Palatine of Chester, in the reign of King John. His descendant was made Viscount Bulkeley in 1643, by King Charles 1 *Lodge's Peerage of Ireland.*

1292: And following years, in the Ragman's Roll or Submission, sworn and subscribed by the nobility and principal gentry of the Scotch nation, to King Edward 1 of England, the following three gentlemen are found:
1. Fergus de Baird, of Meikle and Little Kyp according to Mr. Nisbet, who says it was a great and very considerable family.
2. John Baird, of Evandale, as the same author thinks.
3. Robert Baird. Mr. Nisbet thinks that this was Baird of Cambusnethan, and says that estate went to Sir Alexander Stuart, afterwards of Darnley, by marrying the heiress, Jean Baird, about 1360, and that in 1390 he gave it with his daughter to Sir Thomas Somerville of Carnwath, Lord Somerville's ancestor, upon their marriage.

1296: Duncan, Fergus, John, and Nicol Bairds, all mentioned this year as men of rank and property in *Pryn's Collections*.

1308: Baird of Carnwath, in Clydesdale county of Lanark, with other three or four gentlemen of that name, being convicted of a conspiracy against King Robert Bruce in a Parliament held at Perth, were forfeited, and put to death, and the lands of Carnwath given to Sir Alexander Stuart of Darnley by that Prince. *Dalrymple's Collections*, p.394.

1310: There is a Charter extant, granted by King Robert Bruce to Robert Baird, upon the Barony of Cambusnethan. Ibid.2 This estate lies in the Upper Ward of Clydesdale, county of Lanark. Cambusnethan was long possessed by the Bairds and the late Lord Somerville told me, (Auchmedden) at his own house of Drum, in 1731, that there is a part of the old house still called " The Baird's Tower". [15]

---

[15] Ibid, p. 4

The Gartsherries

By far the oldest remaining family group by place and documentation, the Gartsherries, remnants of the original Cambusnethans, were poor tenant farmers until the eight brothers, sons of Alexander Baird, became wealthy from the efforts of their father and later even more, from hard work themselves. According to the book "The Bairds of Gartsherrie", using documents and papers of Mr. James Baird, the last surviving of the eight original brothers, the compiler wrote:

> *The family has been settled for centuries in Lanarkshire; and there seems no reason to doubt the accuracy of the family tradition that they descended from a younger son of the Cambusnethans.*[16]

These very hardy remnants of the Cambusnethan Bairds began again, as mentioned above, as tenant farmers, but over generations, once again rose to be landowners and wealthy estate farmers, and then moved into industry. They rose in prominence in Old Monkland, and are considered a family of great importance there.[17] It is not known how long the Baird's were in residence at High Cross and Kirkwood Farms, but it must have been a very long time, since no one has memory of when they were not there. The first documentation is of Alexander Baird, born 1659 or there about, and lived at Kirkwood. He was a very powerful man and was called "Double Ribbed Sandy".

---

[16] *The Bairds of Gartsherrie: Their Origin and History.* Glasgow: University Press, 1875, p. 9.
[17] http://www.monklands.co.uk/kirkwood/bairdsofom.htm, retrieved 19 February 2019.

His son, Alexander Baird Jr. continued to work the two farms, and renewed his leases for 19 more years in 1764. He added more lands over time, including Woodhead, and became a very successful farmer. His son, John, continued the farming after the death of this Alexander about 1767. There are documents that show John was farming Kirkwood, his brother Robert farming High Cross, and William at Woodhead, as John's sub-tenants. When the leases were renewed in 1786, the farms were listed as Kirkwood, High Cross, Woodhead, Luggie Bridge, and Waukmill. Waukmill was a mill producing woolen cloth, so the industrial age of the Bairds had begun in earnest, although the last lease of Alexander Jr. listed this mill also.

The younger son, William (1721-1780?), who had been the sub-tenant at Woodhead, became the head of the family when John and Robert died, and continued to farm all the lands, as well as made wool at Waukmill and added more farms over time. He is the father of the Alexander Baird III, who fathered the brothers who made the great fortunes in coal and steel. William's wife and Alexander the III's mother was Jean Baillie. They had four children, Alexander, Helen, John, and William.

Alexander III was born 1765 and died 1833. He was born at Woodhead farm, where his father first farmed as part of the sub-tenancy with his brothers. He then became tenant of Kirkwood and High Cross, as well as Newmains. He married Jean Moffat and had eight sons and two daughters. These sons became the Old Monkland Bairds of Gartsherrie. It is said that Alexander III and Jean had a system of work that was admired by all in the area. They worked long hours, kept the Sabbath, and insisted that their children lead clean, educated, and busy working lives. They expected their children to work alongside, as hard as they did, and were able to achieve a very comfortable life. The children were educated in the neighboring schools, except David, who was given the best education possible in Glasgow, Edinburgh, and Paris.

The children were as follows:
Janet, 6 December 1794; born at Woodhead (Later Janet Wier).
William, 23 April 1796; born at Woodhead (Later William Baird of Elie).
John, 19 February 1798; born at Woodhead. (Later called John Baird of Lochwood and Ury).
Alexander, 29 December 1799; born at Kirkwood (Later Alexander Baird Jr.).
James, 5 December 1802; born at Kirkwood (Later James Baird of Cambusdoon).
Jean, 24 August 1804; born at Kirkwood (Later Jean Jackson).
Robert, 16 April 1806; born at Kirkwood (Later Robert Baird of Auchmedden)
Douglas, 31 March 1808; born at Kirkwood (Later Douglas Baird of Closeburn)
George, 28 July 1810; born at High Cross (Later George Baird of Strichen and Stichill).
David, 18 November 1816 born at High Cross (Later David Buchanan Baird of Stichill).

This fifth generation descending from "Double-Ribbed Sandy", was most industrious indeed. William and James became the iron manufacturers of Gartsherrie, their owned lands there used for the smelting and production of iron products. Several others of the family were involved in their business enterprises. John continued to farm and work with all the lands of the traditional family tenancies, as well as added owned lands. Alexander III had begun a coal mining business in a small way, and Alexander IV (Jr.), the fourth child, was assigned that work, but William also helped with the work and they turned it into one of the largest coal mining operations in Scotland.

Upon the death of their father, William set up the company, William Baird and Company, in partnership with his younger brother James. Their iron works became the largest pig-iron producer in Britain at the time. William and James also enlarged their coal mining operations in Lanarkshire and in Ayrshire. In 1852, James acquired the estate of Greenfield, and renamed it Cambusdoon. Robert bought the old Auchmedden estate in 1853 and lived there until his death.

By the 1870s William Baird & Co were working mines in the North East of England, in what was the county of Cumberland, and also in Spain. In 1893, the firm was incorporated as William Baird & Co Ltd. And in 1931, the company's Ayrshire coal interests were combined with those of the Dalmellington Iron Company in Ayrshire, to form Bairds & Dalmellington Ltd. The new company, seventy-five percent owned by William Baird & Co Ltd, controlled seventy percent of the Ayrshire coalfields. About 1938, the company underwent complete reorganization and entered voluntary liquidation. William Baird & Co Ltd was reconstituted, and the company's Lanarkshire interests merged with the Scottish Iron & Steel Co Ltd, Glasgow, founded in 1912, to form Bairds & Scottish Steel Ltd, pig iron and steel manufacturers.

This merger was directed by Andrew K McCosh, chairman of William Baird & Co Ltd, who saw the mutual benefit in linking up the Northern Steelworks of Scottish Iron & Steel Co Ltd with the Gartsherrie Ironworks of William Baird & Co Ltd. Between 1946 and 1951, the whole of William Baird's coal, iron and steel interests were nationalized, and the company began to diversify into other areas of business, including the textile industry. In 1961, the company merged with Northern Mercantile.

The company continued to diversify and acquired the raincoat manufacturing company, Dannimac Ltd, London, England, in 1981. Then, in 1988 acquired the Windsmoor Group. Between 1992 and 1994, the company disposed of its engineering and building services but in 1994 acquired the Melka and Tenson menswear brands. The company acquired the Lowe Alpine sportswear brand in 1999.

The only current armiger known by this author of the modern Gartsherrie line is Richard Holman-Baird of Rickarton, Ury, and Lochwood. There is another line that remains existent, that of Henry Alexander William Baird of Elie and Durris, who now lives in Australia, and his son, Henry Douglas William Baird is recently interested in matriculating the arms, so is working to do so. His great-grandfather is the last of this line to have matriculated the arms.

The Ordinhivas Bairds

The Ordinhivas Bairds moved north first, but dates are in question. According to J. Malcolm Bulloch, "Migration of the Lanarkshire Bairds then set in. One group, we are told by William Baird, moved northwards to Ross-shire as lairds of Indety and Balmaduthy; and in the fifteenth century one Lanarkshire Baird, having quarreled with a neighbor, is said to have been given sanctuary by the Earl of Huntly, who granted him land in the Forest of Boyne, five centuries ago, in 1430."[18] The Forest of Boyne was a massive expanse of land that reached south and west from Banff in the ancient parishes of both Banff and Fordyce, possibly as far as Aboyne, at that time. This Baird, thought to be James Baird, born about 1400, who

---

[18] J. Malcolm Bulloch, *The Bairds of Auchmedden and Strichen, Aberdeenshire*. Buchan Club, Peterhead: Scotland, 1934, p 2.

married a Kerr, daughter of Robert Kerr, lived in the Forest of Boyne and his sons continued to move north.

The Boyne group continued moving to Ordinhivas or Ordinhuiff, it is believed, lands which later became a part of the Seafield Estates of Fordyce, and it was reported by William Baird, 7th Laird of Auchmedden, that Thomas Baird, b. 1440, was the son of James Baird, "Baillie of Banff", married to Elizabeth Gordon and born about 1415. This James the Baillie was the son of the first James Baird of Boyne, and lived at Banff, but his place of death is unknown. James the Baillie married Elizabeth Gordon, a daughter of John Gordon, in 1436. Her death place is also unknown.

Their son, Thomas Baird, was born about 1440, and married Helen Urquhart in 1463. His son, Thomas Baird, 1st of Ordinhivas, was also the "Ballie at Banff" and married Janet Maitland in 1490. Their son, George, 2nd of Ordinhivas, was the father of William, according to the McFarlane Genealogy[19], but was the father of Walter, according to J. Malcom Bulloch[20]. William the 7th Laird of Auchmedden's notes skip this William and go straight to Walter. We mention it here as a reminder that we are working with ancient texts and records and sometimes they are juxtaposed against other records. We in the 21st century cannot possibly know what really happened so many centuries ago. We will leave it to the acceptance that we can only do what we can with tracing our lines, so for this history, we will leave both this William and Walter in place. One or the other is the son or the grandson of George. It seems that William only lived from 1515-1539, so it is possible he is the father of Walter, but George and

---

[19] Clan McFarlane Genealogy.
[20] J. Malcolm Bulloch, *The Bairds of Auchmedden and Strichen, Aberdeenshire*. Buchan Club, Peterhead: Scotland, 1934, p 3.

his wife reared Walter after his father died. Walter was born before 1539, according to records, and died 14 December 1589. We know that tiny bit, and Walter was called the 3rd of Ordinhivas, possibly because the William in question never received his title due to having died prior to his own father. It is also possible this father William died before Walter was born, thus the confusion as to which man/generation was the actual father.

    Walter was the first Baird historically called "Chief of the Name" in documents and letters within the family. This is extremely important because this shows that the Bairds of Auchmedden were not the first considered "chief". In actuality, the first named "Chief" was a Baird who moved to the north from Lanarkshire, not by way of Posso. Walter's wife was Catherine Grant of Ballindalloch, daughter of John Grant of Ballindalloch, as well as the widow of Alexander, 2nd Laird of Kinninvie. The marriage of their only known child, Lillias, was where the Ordinhivas and Auchmedden Bairds came back together to continue the lines. Again, Walter died in 1589; Lillias married Gilbert Baird, 3rd of Auchmedden, 16 August 1578, and died 2 April 1624, presumably on the estate of Auchmedden, or at the house in Banff used by the family during the winter months. Gilbert the 3rd of Auchmedden died 23 February 1620, most likely in Banff. It is reported that these two had thirty-two children and populated Bairds to all the North of Scotland. It is sure they did not have thirty-two natural children, but there was and still is a system of "fostering" in the highlands, and it is suspected that many of these children were acquired in that fashion.

"Boyne, an ancient thanedom, an ancient forest, and a burn, in Banffshire. The thanedom comprised the chief part of Boyndie parish, and certain parts of Banff and Fordyce parishes; belonged, in the time of Robert Bruce, to Randolph, Earl of Murray; and passed

subsequently to the Ogilvies, ancestors of the Earl of Seafield. The forest comprehended a large district on the E and the S of Fordyce parish; included also Blairmaud in Boyndie parish; lay strictly contiguous to the thanedom; and stretched both E and W of the Forester's Seat at Tarbreich, on the shunk of Bin Hill of Cullen. The burn rises in Fordyce parish on the northern slope of Knock Hill at 730 feet above sea-level, and thence flows 9¾ miles north-north-eastward, chiefly along the Boyndie boundary to Boyne Bay."[21]

The Posso Bairds

The Posso Bairds of Pebbleshire first appeared through documents in 1487, when a William Bard "de Posso" witnessed a charter. It is not proven where the Posso Bairds came from, but there is a Gilbert as a name of Bairds of Kilkenzie and Kilkerren in the Earldom of Carrick, Ayrshire, at the beginning of the 16th century, so there may have been a connection between the Posso's and the Lanarkshire Bairds.[22] Unfortunately, there are few written documents prior to the 15th century, and those few do not describe family relationships well. Many of this line claim Thomas de Bard, sheriff of Posso, who is believed to have died by 1296, as their ancestor, but documents are lacking. Posso and the area of Lanarkshire where Bairds lived were very close together, and the Possos appeared after the Cambusnethans of Lanark, so it is reasonable to believe the two were related, or the Possos were descended from the Cambusnethans. Also, there was a place called "Auchmedden" in Lanark, between the Cambusnethans and the Possos, but it has been proven the Auchmedden of the north was named before Andrew Baird arrived, so

---

[21] Frances Groome. *Ordnance Gazetteer of Scotland,* 1882-85, p. 183
[22] Ibid.

it cannot be assumed that he named it thus. It may have been that he was aware of the other Auchmedden when he purchased the estate.

Regardless of ties to the Cambusnethans or no, Gilbert Baird of Posso reared his family in the borders of Scotland, located about five and a half miles south-west of Pebbles. His claimed forbear, Thomas de Bard, sheriff of Peebles in 1296, was able to gain restoration of his lands after having sworn fealty to Edward I of England, also known as Longshanks and the Hammer of the Scots. His son Thomas was given a charter for the lands of Posso by Robert III, King of the Scots and the line continued down to Gilbert, who was killed at the Battle of Flodden in 1513.

This Gilbert had two sons, John, who inherited Posso, and Andrew, later of Lavorklaw, and then Auchmedden in Aberdeenshire. John of Posso married Janet Scott and had two daughters, ending the male line of Posso. John's lands went to the Nasmyth's, the eldest daughter Elizabeth having married Thomas Michael Nasmyth.[23] Little more is known of the Posso group, other than the remaining son of the Posso Bairds was Andrew, who came to Auchmedden.

The Auchmedden Bairds

Memorial of George Baird reads: Here lies the honourable GEORGE BAIRDE of Auchmedden who d. 29.5.1593 in his 76th year.[24] George Baird of Auchmeddan, Banffshire. Married to Elizabeth Keith. Parents: Andrew Baird (____ - 1543) Children: Gilbert Baird (____ - 1620)
James, 5th Laird later had this inscription added: 1559 - JAMES BAIRD of Auchmedden erected this monument to the memory of his predecessors: ANDREW, GEORGE, GILBERT and GEORGE BAIRD, whose ashes are

---

[23] William N. Fraser, *An Account of the Surname of Baird: particularly of the families of Auchmedden, Newbyth and Saughtonhall*. Stevens: Edinburgh, 1857, p 3.
[24] Jervaise. *Aberdeenshire Epitaphs and Inscriptions*, Vol 1, p 56, transcribed from the Latin.

here interred. They died respectively 10.2.1543, 29 May 1593, 23 Feb 1620 and 12 Feb 1642. The ashes of ANNE FRASER and ELIZABETH KEITH, his mother and great-grandmother, likewise lie here interred.

Andrew Baird, 1st Laird of Auchmedden, son of Gilbert of Posso, left Posso when his part of the family lost most of its holdings, due to debt. The senior line of the Posso Bairds had ended in two daughters, one who married Thomas Michael Nasmyth and the other William Geddes. Near the middle of the sixteenth century, the Posso estate was halved and went to the Nasmyth and Hay of Smeithfield families. At this juncture, with little left for him at home, Andrew moved to Fife and first is found in records as the Laird of Scotscraig. In November 1534, he bought Auchmedden on the Buchan Coast. Andrew's descendants held Auchmedden until it was sold, just before being taken by the Hanoverians, by William the 7th and last Baird Laird of the name. [25]

The son of Andrew, George, 2nd Laird, took over at the death of his father in 1543. George married Protestants, but was an ardent Catholic, and attended Huntly at the Battle of Corrichie, 1562. He was also present at the "Insurrection of Aberdeen" in 1589, on the Catholic side, and paid heavy fines for his activities. He was pardoned by the king, who pretended to believe his being involved was a mistake. Regardless, he was married to Elizabeth Keith, the daughter of Gilbert Keith of Troup, the son of the 3rd Earl Marischal. It probably did not hurt that he had such strong ties to the Court of the time. Richard Holman-Baird, our current commander is also directly descended from William Keith, the 3rd Earl Marischal, which makes him related to the Auchmedden Bairds through Walter Baird of Ordinhivas and the Keith's.

---

[25] J. Malcolm Bulloch, *The Bairds of Auchmedden and Strichen, Aberdeenshire*. Buchan Club, Peterhead, Scotland, 1934, p 4.

This George died in 1593, and his son, Gilbert, 3rd Laird of Auchmedden began his work. He married Lillias Baird of Ordinhivas, considered a distant cousin, and was reported to be an absolute Catholic who would not yield. Gilbert brought two of the Baird lines back together with Lillias. They had numerous children, and their eldest son, George, 4th Laird, became sheriff of Banff, living more in Banff than at Auchmedden. There was a large house in the town, where the Bairds spent most all winters.

George, the 4th Laird, became sheriff of Banff in 1634 and was identified as a part of Banff more than Auchmedden. He fought first on the Catholic side of the Civil War, but then traded to the Covenanters in 1640. His son, James, the 5th Laird, took over when George died in 1642. It seems James had a great deal of natural ability and looks, as well as good head for business and added much to the lands held by the family. In 1658 he became sheriff of Banffshire. His grandson, James Baird, 6th Laird, took over at this death in 1691. This James' son, also named James, died in 1681 and never attained his title.

James was very influential and was responsible, along with Alexander Garden of Troup, for building the bridge that still stands at the formerly named Mill of Auchmedden, now Mill of Nethermill, on the border between Aberdeenshire and Banffshire, as well as Gamrie and Aberdour parishes. It was the first bridge ever built that would allow wagons and commerce between the towns, other than what could be carried on the backs of horses or man or go far inland to cross. This bridge was built in 1719, due to government pressure for large landowners to improve the roads in the highlands.

James was succeeded by his son William Baird, the 7th Laird of Auchmedden, and the last. William was involved in helping Lord Lewis Gordon and James Moir of Stonywood raise troops for Prince Charles Edward Stewart, the "Bonnie Prince" as well was reported at his side during the rising of 1745. This William was forced to sell Auchmedden for the debts incurred and his children dispersed. The Auchmedden Bairds remained Catholic, even when they had to pay heavy fines for doing so, which is another clue that they identified as fully highlander by this time. Although they never wrote formal letters in Gaelic, it is believed that they spoke and wrote it, in order to communicate with those who worked their farms and lands on and off the estate. They used Latin and English, as well as French, in letters between family members, showing that they were well educated and preferred to write in those languages used by the educated of the time.

The Bairds of Auchmedden immigrated to the new world, to the British Navy, and to France as monks, but the family never reassembled in Scotland, and William the 7th, as well as his wife Anne, died in Aberdeen, penniless and at the mercy of her brother, William, Earl of Fife. It was the influence of the Earl that gained William, 7th Laird of Auchmedden, a pardon from the King and the right to remain in Scotland after the rising. William spent the rest of his life writing the history of the Bairds, as he knew it. It has been impossible to find his sons who moved to Antiqua and Barbuda in the Virgin Islands, and their families may have moved on to the continental United States, but to date, they have not been identified.

The Newbyths

The fourth son of Gilbert, 3rd Laird of Auchmedden, James, bought the lands of Byth in Gamrie Parish and when he moved south, changed the name of his new estate to Newbyth. James was to become Lord Deveron but died before the patents passed the seal, in 1655. His eldest son, John Baird, became a Lord of Session, Lord Newbyth, and his son William was created a baronet of Nova Scotia before John's death, the first Baron of Newbyth. John died in 1698.

Sir John, who was knighted and styled himself as Lord Newbyth, inherited his father's lands in Byth, Aberdeenshire, but found them to be remote, preferring the Newbyth lands closer to Edinburgh, adding to them greatly. His son, Sir William Baird, 1st Baronet (1654-1737), built a large new house on the estate in the early 18th century. Sir William's eldest son, Sir John (1685-1745) inherited the title and the lands, but died not long after his father, and the baronetcy became extinct, the lands passing to a grandson of Robert Baird, the 1st Baronet of Saughtonhall.

This grandson was William Baird, (1697-1765), the second cousin to Sir John, 2nd Baronet of the original line. William inherited Newbyth, and his son unexpectedly died shortly after him, so the estate passed to the younger brother, Robert (1752-1828). The house stood until 1813, when it was gutted by fire. Robert had it pulled down and built a new house, designed by Alexander Elliot. Robert's younger brother, General Sir David Baird (1757-1829, of great military fame), was made baronet in his own right, 1st Baronet of the 3rd Creation, but had no heirs, so his brother Robert's son, David (1795-1852), became Sir David Baird, 2nd Baronet. In 1852, the Newbyth estate was passed to another Sir David Baird (1831-1913), 3rd Baronet. He was also a soldier, but for just eight years. The next was Sir David Baird (1865-1941), 4th Baronet, who had a difficult time keeping the estate and house well provided for, and he had no heirs. He had the estate and baronetcy made over to his brother William Arthur Baird, who had inherited from his mother's father, much more than Sir David had inherited as the first-born. Regardless, he outlived his brother William, and the baronetcy was inherited by his nephew, another Sir David Baird (1912-2000), 5th Baronet. The current, and 6th Baronet of the 3rd Creation, is the nephew of the 5th Baronet, and is Sir Charles William Stuart Baird, who currently resides in Australia. It is not certain whether Sir Charles William

Stuart Baird has matriculated his arms. The Newbyth lands and estates were sold after World War Two, which saw the end of three centuries of Baird holdings for this line. The heir apparent, Andrew James Baird of England, is a fourth cousin of Sir Charles William Stuart Baird.

The Saughtonhalls

The Saughtonhalls are also descendants of James, the fourth son of Gilbert, 3rd of Auchmedden. The barony was set up through James' second son, Robert Baird of Saughtonhall, who was made a baronet of Nova Scotia in 1696. He died the following year, and his estates and titles passed to his eldest son Sir James Baird, 2nd Baronet (1657-1715). He was succeeded by his eldest son, Sir Robert Baird (1684-1740), 3rd Baronet. His eldest son, Sir David Baird (1716-45), 4th Baronet, died childless in the Battle of Fontenoy. The Baronetcy then passed to his younger brother, Sir William Baird, (1721-1771), 5th Baronet, a career soldier who made little use of the house or the estate. He married Frances Gardiner, whose father had died in the battle of Prestonpans, although he was not directly in the fight, but died in the firefight around his house at Bankton. Their son, Lt. Col. Sir James Gardiner Baird, 6th Baronet (1756-1830), lived in the house for a while when his children were young, but preferred better housing and rented out the house to become a lunatic asylum. He was famous for his military feats for the English during the American Revolutionary War. The Saughtonhall Bairds have a generational history of being soldiers of the highest honor and quality.

His grandson, also Sir James Gardiner Baird, 7th Baronet (1813-1896), also a career soldier, lived at many addresses in Edinburgh, continuing to lease out the estate, but the Edinburgh suburbs were moving in, and his son, Sir William James Gardiner

Baird, 8th Baronet (1854-1921) sold most of the land for housing development. The mental hospital in the house closed in 1907, and the house was sold to Edinburgh Corporation, in a sorry state indeed. After World War II, it was in a state of dry rot, and was burned as a spectacle on Guy Fawkes Day, 1952, for the city celebration, the remains being taken up and made into the roads of the city. The heir apparent to this line is Sir James Andrew Gardiner Baird, who is still living, but has not, to date, claimed his title of 11th Baronet nor matriculated his arms.

Bairds Have Never Been Part of Another Clan, nor a Sept

Bairds have not been claimed by, nor have they agreed to be a part of another clan or family; even after the great diaspora. They have remained independent through the years after Culloden, but fractured. Bairds are fierce in their love of name and Scotland. Those who are part of the diaspora cling to the stories told by parents, grandparents and great-grandparents. These Bairds have a collective memory of what "was" in Scotland and wish to know the modern Scotland as they do the stories passed down to them. It has been far too long, and a leader from amongst us is most severely needed, to bring the diasporic and Scottish family members together in service to the whole Baird Family worldwide.

Bairds Are Considered a Separate and Distinct Family, Under a Chief of Name and Arms

The Bairds, as a family, have a leader once again. In the post-modern world, while so many people are displaced and refugees from so many ills of the world, it is of utmost importance that a Scottish family have a leader. A leader of Bairds must be able to work with all Bairds. A modern leader/Clan Commander/Chief should be able to promote the interests of the Bairds and of Scotland at all levels of society. This person should be willing to expend his/her assets to further the goals of the entire Baird family, not just his or her line. A Commander/Chief needs excellent communication, diplomatic, and team-oriented skills that may not have been required in earlier eras. Clan Baird needs someone who can respectfully and successfully work with all people, one who can represent family interests in Scotland as well as other areas of the world where we live in large numbers, and one who understands the timeline of our family history. It is also important for our chief or commander to have a presence in Scotland, in order to develop opportunities for our homeland and our family. These opportunities may be educational, artistic, cultural, economic, or simply historic. Since so many of us live in other parts of the world, this presence in Scotland is much more important than other attributes. That connection is vital in our search for a leader. Leadership in Scotland will also provide a center for Bairds to congregate in the future, and will provide for Scotland herself to inherit the benefits of all the Baird family's combined energy and resources.

On 19 August 2019, The Lord Lyon King of Arms, Dr. Joseph Morrow, appointed Richard Holman-Baird as our Commander, for a period of five years. We finally have a leader again, after nearly three-hundred years. Richard is a Baird through this Gartsherrie Lanarkshire line, and through the Keiths, coming down from Elizabeth Keith, wife of Gilbert, Laird of Auchmedden, and their many sons. A copy of the appointment is on the next page.

Warrant

from

Lord Lyon King of Arms

in the application of

Debra J. Baird, Ph.D, residing at 3491 County Road 3459, Hayleyville, Alabama, and Others, for the Appointment of RICHARD HOLMAN-BAIRD OF RICKARTON, URY AND LOCHWOOD to be the Commander of the Honourable Clan Baird

of date 5 August 2019

Edinburgh, 19 August 2019; The Lord Lyon King of Arms, having considered the foregoing Petition Grants Warrant to the Lyon Clerk to prepare a Commission appointing the said Richard Holman-Baird of Rickarton, Ury and Lochwood to be Commander of the Honourable Clan Baird for a period of five years.

Arms and Armigers

The earliest arms of Baird are recorded in the Slains armorial as:

Vert, on a fess Argent between three mullets in chief Or and a boar statant in base Or, an eagle's head erased Sable.[26]

This is considerably different than the listing in Mackenzie's *Scotland's Herauldrie* (1680) as:

Gules a Board Passant Or for Baird of Auchmedden, and for Baird of Newbyth (1st Creation); Gules, and on a Canton Ermine, A sword in pale proper. [27]

The above contrasts dramatically against the description provided by the Carrick Pursuivant, MacDonald in 1904 in his work *Scottish Armorial Seals* where he gives the armorial seal for Andrew Baird as:

Andrew, ' in Scottiscrag.' A shield, parted per pale, bearing arms: Dexter: A lion rampant. Sinister: A chevron between three (stars or boar heads erased?). Legend (Goth. I.e.): & antom batfc. Diam. in. Reg. Ho. Ch. 15 May 1534.

As well as:

BAIRD, Andrew, of Auchmedden, same as above. 1st and 4th: A lion (passant or rampant?). 2nd and 3rd: Three (wolf or boar) heads erased. Legend (Goth. I.e.): JS antim bartf. Diam. in. Reg. Ho. Ch. 3 Nov. 1537, do. 20 Nov. 1537. [28]

All of the above show that prior to the Lyon register, the Baird arms

---

[26] http://www.heraldry-scotland.co.uk/slains.html. SL 186. Retrieved 20 July 2019.

[27] http://www.heraldry-scotland.co.uk/mackenzie.html. Retrieved 20 July 2019.

[28] McDonald, William Rae (Carrick Pursuivant). *Scottish Armorial Seals*. William Green and Sons, Edinburgh, 1904.

altered dramatically to the point that attempting to show descent prior to the Lyon register solely on Armorial bearing is a difficult if not impossible task.

DNA

Baird (etc.) results from online DNA Project[28] show a wide variety in DNA traces. Genetics DNA databases always come with the issue of self-selection and low sampling but the distribution shows that there are dramatic differences in markers presented. Including the presence of (haplogroups E, I), but the majority who have tested at a decent number of markers fall into M-269, also called R1b1a2 or the R1A group. R1b is the most common Y-haplogroup in Western Europe, and the most common sub-group in R1b is M269. The frequency is about 92% in Wales, 82% in Ireland (as high as 95% in some parts of Ireland), 70% in Scotland, 68% in Spain, 60% in France (76% in Normandy), 45% in Eastern England, 50% in Germany, 50% in the Netherlands, 42% in Iceland, 43% in Denmark, and so on.

A Baird Bibliography

Bulloch, J. Malcolm, *The Bairds of Auchmedden and Strichen, Aberdeenshire*. (Peterhead: Scotland, Buchan Club, 1934).

Cheape, Hugh and Grant I.F. *Periods in Highland History*. (New York, Barnes and Noble, 1997). ISBN: 0-7607-1715-X.

Clan McFarlane Genealogy. https://www.clanmacfarlanegenealogy.info/, retrieved 10 February 2019.

Forbes, Robert. *The Lyon in Mourning: or A Collection of speeches, letters, journals, etc. relative to the affairs of Prince Charles Edward Stuart*. (Edinburgh, University Press, 1895).

Fraser, William N., *An Account of the Surname of Baird: particularly of the families of Auchmedden, Newbyth and Saughtonhall*. (Edinburgh, Stevens, 1857).

Grimble, Ian. *Clans and Chiefs, Celtic Tribalism in Scotland*. (Edinburgh, Birlinn Ltd., 1980). ISBN: 0-7607-2269-2.

Grimble, Ian. *Scottish Clans and Tartans*. (New York, Hamlyn Publishing, 1973). ISBN: 0-8148-0570-1.

Groome, Frances. *Ordnance Gazetteer of Scotland,* 1882-85.

http://www.monklands.co.uk/kirkwood/bairdsofom.htm, retrieved 19 February 2019.

http://www.heraldry-scotland.co.uk/slains.html. SL 186. Retrieved 20 July 2019.

http://www.heraldry-scotland.co.uk/mackenzie.html, retrieved 20 July 2019.

Jackson, Kenneth Hurlstone. *A Celtic Miscellany, A Collection of Classic Celtic Literature*. (New York, Penguin Books, 1971, revised edition). ISBN: 0-88029-095-1.

Jervaise. *Aberdeenshire Epitaphs and Inscriptions*. (Vol1, transcribed from the Latin).

Kingsley, Nick. *Landed Families of Britain and Ireland Blog, article 329, Baird of Newbyth and Saughtonhall, baronets.* (http://landedfamilies.blogspot.com/2018/05/329-baird-of-newbyth-and-saughtonhall.html, 7 May 2018).

MacBain, Alexander. *An Etymological dictionary of the Gaelic language*. (Stirling, Eneas Mackay, 1911).

MacDonald, Micheil. *The Clans of Scotland, The History and Landscape of the Scottish Clans*. (Edison, NJ, Chartwell Books, 1994). ISBN: 0-7858-0108-1.

McDonald, William Rae (Carrick Pursuivant). *Scottish Armorial Seals*. (Edinburgh, William Green and Sons,1904).

MacKinnon, Charles. *The Scottish Highlanders, A Personal View*. (New York, St. Martins Press, 1984). ISBN: 0-312- 70505-0.

Maclean, Fitzroy. *Highlanders, A History of the Scottish Clans*. (New York, Penguin Books, 1995). ISBN: 0-670-86644- X.

Mason, Gordon W. *The Castles of Glasgow and Clyde*. 2nd ed. (Goblinshead, 2014). ISBN: 9-781899874-59-0.

McDonald, R. Andrew. *The Kingdom of the Isles, Scotland's Western Seaboard, c. 1100-c.1336*. (East Linton, Scotland, Tuckwell Press, 1997). ISBN: 1-898410-85-2.

McIan, R.R. *The Clans of the Scottish Highlands*. (London, Chancellor Press, 1983, first published 1845). ISBN: 0- 907486-38-X.

Private Author. *The Bairds of Gartsherrie: Their Origin and History.* (Glasgow, University Press, 1875).

Ragman's Rolls Index (Edinburgh, Bannatyne Club, 1834).

Tayler, Alistair Norwich. *The Book of the Duffs, Compiled by Alistair and Henrietta Tayler.* (Edinburgh, William Brown, 1914).

The Chartulary of Glasgow, (Scotch College at Paris).

Thomson, Derick S. *The New English-Gaelic Dictionary*. (Glasgow, Gairm Publications, 1999). ISBN: 1-871901-32-4.

Zaczek, Iain. *World Tartans*. (London, Collins & Brown, 2001). ISBN: 0-7607-2589-6.

www.ingramcontent.com/pod-product-compliance
Lightning Source LLC
Chambersburg PA
CBHW041812040426
42450CB00001B/13